KEEP CALM YOU'RE ONLY 21
KEEP CALM YOU'RE ONLY 21
KEEP CALM YOU'RE ONLY 21
KEEP CALM YOU'RE ONLY 21
KEEP CALM YOU'RE ONLY 21
KEEP CALM YOU'RE ONLY 21
KEEP CALM YOU'RE ONLY 21
KEEP CALM YOU'RE ONLY 21

KEEP
CALM

YOU'RE ONLY

KEEP CALM YOU'RE ONLY 21

Copyright © Summersdale Publishers Ltd, 2012

With text contributed by Yvette Jane

Summersdale Publishers Ltd
46 West Street
Chichester
West Sussex
PO19 1RP
UK

www.summersdale.com

Printed and bound in the Czech Republic

ISBN: 978-1-84953-361-4

Substantial discounts on bulk quantities of Summersdale books are available to corporations, professional associations and other organisations. For details contact Summersdale Publishers by telephone: +44 (0) 1243 771107, fax: +44 (0) 1243 786300 or email: nicky@summersdale.com.

KEEP
CALM

YOU'RE ONLY

21

summersdale

CONTENTS

ANOTHER
YEAR
OLDER

Finally twenty-one, and
legally able to do everything
I've been doing since fifteen.

Anonymous

My mother is going to
have to stop lying about
her age because pretty soon
I'm going to be older
than she is.

Tripp Evans

Real birthdays are
not annual affairs.
Real birthdays are
the days when we
have a new birth.

Ralph Parlette

I'm not sure
I'm adult yet.

Johnny Depp

Birth may be a matter
of a moment, but it is
a unique one.

Frederick Leboyer

Whatever with the
past has gone,
The best is always
yet to come.

Lucy Larcom

The best birthdays of all
are those that haven't
arrived yet.

Robert Orben

All the world is a birthday cake, so take a piece, but not too much.

George Harrison

To remain young
one must change.

Alexander Chase

The other day a man asked
me what I thought was the
best time of life. 'Why,'
I answered… 'Now.'

David Grayson

From our birthday,
until we die,
Is but the winking
of an eye.

William Butler Yeats

There must be a day or two in a man's life when he is the precise age for something important.

Franklin Pierce Adams

For years I wanted
to be older, and
now I am.

Margaret Atwood

… there was a star danced,
and under that was I born.

William Shakespeare,
Much Ado about Nothing

Youth comes but
once in a lifetime.

Henry Wadsworth Longfellow

I think all this talk about age
is foolish. Every time I'm
one year older, everyone
else is too.

Gloria Swanson

JUST
WHAT
I
ALWAYS
WANTED

Celebrate all the things you don't like about yourself – love yourself.

Lady Gaga

I know I want to have
children while my parents
are still young enough to
take care of them.

Rita Rudner

Some people wanted
champagne and caviar
when they should have had
beer and hot dogs.

Dwight D. Eisenhower

Ask for what you want
and be prepared
to get it!

Maya Angelou

I have always felt a
gift diamond shines so
much better than one
you buy for yourself.

Mae West

The more you praise
and celebrate your
life, the more there is
in life to celebrate.

Oprah Winfrey

All my life, I always wanted to be somebody. Now I see that I should have been more specific.

Jane Wagner

If only we'd stop
trying to be happy
we could have a
pretty good time.

Edith Wharton

My present was a cake.
Ablaze with so many
candles, I fully expected
to see boy scouts camped
around it.

Anonymous

I like wearing
necklaces, because
it lets me know when
I'm upside down.

Mitch Hedberg

Life isn't tied with a
bow, but it's still a gift.

Anonymous

Birthdays are nature's
way of telling you to
eat more cake.

Jo Brand

The Lord loveth a cheerful giver. He also accepteth from a grouch.

Catherine Hall

Happiness never decreases by being shared.

Buddha

When you know what
you want, and want it bad
enough, you will find a
way to get it.

Jim Rohn

GREAT
EXPECTATIONS

Be careful whose toes
you step on today because
they might be connected
to the foot that kicks your
ass tomorrow!

Anonymous

Nearly all the best
things that came
to me in life have
been unexpected,
unplanned by me.

Carl Sandburg

If we all did the things
we are capable of doing,
we would literally astound
ourselves.

Thomas Edison

When someone asks
if you'd like cake or
pie, why not say you
want cake and pie?

Lisa Loeb

The highest reward for
a person's toil is not what
they get for it, but what
they become by it.

John Ruskin

Find out what you
like doing best and
get someone to pay
you for doing it.

Katharine Whitehorn

Experience tells you what to do; confidence allows you to do it.

Stan Smith

A lot of fellows nowadays
have a B.A., M.D. or Ph.D.
Unfortunately, they don't
have a J.O.B.

Fats Domino

The young do not know
enough to be prudent... so
they attempt the impossible,
and achieve it, generation
after generation.

Pearl S. Buck

Nothing succeeds
like the appearance
of success.

Christopher Lasch

The closest to perfection a person ever comes is when he fills out a job application form.

Stanley J. Randall

If you hear a voice within
you say 'you cannot paint',
then by all means paint, and
that voice will be silenced.

Vincent van Gogh

You can't put off
being young until
you retire.

Philip Larkin

Adults are always asking little kids what they want to be when they grow up because they're looking for ideas.

Paula Poundstone

Only undertake what you can do in an excellent fashion. There are no prizes for average performance.

Brian Tracy

Youth is the best time
to be rich, and the
best time to be poor.

Anonymous

SEIZE
THE
DAY

To change one's life:
Start immediately. Do it
flamboyantly. No exceptions.

William James

If at first you don't
succeed, skydiving
is not for you.

Arthur McAuliff

As a job seeker,
remember this: You only
lack experience if they want
it done the same old way.

Robert Brault

Age considers;
youth ventures.

Rabindranath Tagore

Between two evils,
I generally like to pick the
one I never tried before.

Mae West

The only person who is educated is the one who has learned how to learn and change.

Carl Rogers

Zeal, n. A certain
nervous disorder
afflicting the young
and inexperienced.

Ambrose Bierce

Learning is not attained by
chance, it must be sought
for with ardour and attended
to with diligence.

Abigail Adams

What you need isn't
always what you want.

Robert Jordan

The follies which a man
regrets most in his life
are those which he didn't
commit when he had the
opportunity.

Helen Rowland

You will never find
time for anything.
If you want time you
must make it.

Charles Buxton

Happiness is the meaning
and the purpose of life,
the whole aim and end of
human existence.

Aristotle

Youth is the time for the adventures of the body, but age for the triumphs of the mind.

Logan Pearsall Smith

Why always 'not yet'?
Do flowers in spring
say 'not yet'?

Norman Douglas

Decide then whether or
not the goal is worth the
risks involved. If it is,
stop worrying.

Amelia Earhart

Education is not preparation for life; education is life itself.

John Dewey

Don't be fooled by the calendar. There are only as many days in the year as you make use of.

Charles Richards

OLD
ENOUGH
TO KNOW
BETTER

Old enough to know better,
pissed enough not to care.

Sherrilyn Kenyon

I can resist everything
except temptation.

Oscar Wilde

Interestingly, young people don't come to you for advice. Especially the ones who are related to you.

Meryl Streep

The older you get the
more important it is
not to act your age.

Ashleigh Brilliant

Nobody knows the age
of the human race, but
everybody agrees that it is
old enough to know better.

Anonymous

Nobody can make
you feel inferior without
your consent.

Eleanor Roosevelt

Real knowledge is to
know the extent of
one's ignorance.

Confucius

Do the best you can until you know better. Then when you know better, do better.

Maya Angelou

We are young
only once, after
that we need some
other excuse.

Anonymous

Sometimes the questions
are complicated and the
answers are simple.

Dr Seuss

As long as you know
men are like children,
you know everything.

Coco Chanel

A man who is old enough
to know better is always
on the lookout for a girl
who doesn't.

Anonymous

I don't believe you
should make fun of
anyone but yourself.

Cameron Diaz

Lead me not into temptation; I can find it myself.

Anonymous

Giving up smoking is the
easiest thing in the world.
I know because I've done it
thousands of times.

Mark Twain

My experience is that as soon as people are old enough to know better, they don't know anything at all.

Oscar Wilde

MEASURING
MATURITY

Those are my principles.
If you don't like them
I have others.

Groucho Marx

The only source of knowledge is experience.

Albert Einstein

Young men are as apt
to think themselves wise
enough, as drunken men
are to think themselves
sober enough.

Lord Chesterfield

I spent a lot of money on booze, birds and fast cars – the rest I just squandered.

George Best

The older I grow the more I
distrust the familiar doctrine
that age brings wisdom.

H. L. Mencken

Nobody who ever
gave his best
regretted it.

George Halas

There is only one
person who could ever
make you happy, and
that person is you.

David Burns

When you're young, try
to be realistic; as you get
older, become idealistic.
You'll live longer.

Anthony J. D'Angelo

Few women admit
their age. Few men
act theirs.

Anonymous

I hate that word,
mature, but I guess
I am growing up.

Sheryl Crow

Many of life's failures
are people who did
not realise how close
they were to success
when they gave up.

Thomas Edison

A diamond cannot be
polished without friction,
nor a man perfected
without trials.

Chinese proverb

True, a little learning
is a dangerous thing,
but it still beats total
ignorance.

Abigail Van Buren

The rate at which a person can mature is directly proportional to the embarrassment he can tolerate.

Douglas Engelbart

THE
DATING
GAME

Sex without love is merely
healthy exercise.

Robert A. Heinlein

Any man who can drive
safely while kissing a pretty
girl is simply not giving
the kiss the attention
it deserves.

Albert Einstein

Dating is more than a cup of coffee and less than signing a lease.

Sharon Romm

Sex appeal is 50 per cent
what you've got and
50 per cent what people
think you've got.

Sophia Loren

I have such poor
vision I can date
anybody.

Garry Shandling

Celebrate love. It is
the breath of your existence
and the best of all reasons
for living.

Anonymous

Save a boyfriend for
a rainy day – and
another, in case it
doesn't rain.

Mae West

No man is worth your tears,
but once you find one that
is, he won't make you cry.

Anonymous

A pair of powerful
spectacles has
sometimes sufficed to
cure a person in love.

Friedrich Nietzsche

Computer dating
is fine, if you're a
computer.

Rita Mae Brown

Always remember this: 'A kiss will never miss, and after many kisses a miss becomes a misses.'

John Lennon

You don't love someone for their looks, or their clothes, or for their fancy car, but because they sing a song only you can hear.

Anonymous

I've been on so many
blind dates, I should
get a free dog.

Wendy Liebman

God made woman
beautiful and foolish;
beautiful, that man might
love her, and foolish, that
she might love him.

Anonymous

A man on a date wonders if he'll get lucky. The woman already knows.

Monica Piper

Dating is pressure and tension. What is a date, really, but a job interview that lasts all night.

Jerry Seinfeld

The best way to find
your perfect match is
to meet love halfway.

Anonymous

FIT
FOR
LIFE

Physical fitness can neither
be achieved by wishful
thinking nor outright
purchase.

Joseph Pilates

Smile;
it's free therapy.

Doug Horton

You've gotta keep fit to play
that hard every night. Better
order five more beers.

James Hetfield

I have to exercise in the morning before my brain figures out what I'm doing.

Marsha Doble

Fashion is what you
adopt when you don't
know who you are.

Quentin Crisp

Aerobics: A series of strenuous exercises which help convert fats, sugars and starches into aches, pains and cramps.

Anonymous

Clothes and manners
do not make the man;
but, when he is made,
they greatly improve
his appearance.

Henry Ward Beecher

Fitness –
if it came in a bottle,
everybody would have
a great body.

Cher

The only exercise some people get is jumping to conclusions, running down their friends, side-stepping responsibility and pushing their luck!

Anonymous

The only rule is
don't be boring…
Dress cute wherever
you go, life is too
short to blend in.

Paris Hilton

I don't exercise. If God had wanted me to bend over, he would have put diamonds on the floor.

Joan Rivers

Of all the things you wear,
your expression is the
most important.

Anonymous

My idea of exercise
is a good brisk sit.

Phyllis Diller

Appearances are not held to be a clue to the truth… But we seem to have no other.

Ivy Compton-Burnett

Exercise should be regarded as tribute to the heart.

Gene Tunney

'Style' is an expression of individualism mixed with charisma. 'Fashion' is something that comes after style.

John Fairchild

Exercise is a dirty
word. Every time
I hear it, I wash
my mouth out with
chocolate.

Anonymous

THE
WORLD
IS YOUR
OYSTER

Put your future in good
hands – your own.

Anonymous

If what you're working for
really matters, you'll give it
all you've got.

Nido Qubein

... I'm not afraid
of storms, for I'm
learning how to sail
my ship.

Louisa May Alcott

Keep away from people who
try to belittle your ambitions.
Small people always do
that, but the really great
make you feel that you, too,
can become great.

Mark Twain

Use your imagination
not to scare yourself
to death but to inspire
yourself to life.

Adele Brookman

Success comes in cans, not can'ts.

Anonymous

Never be afraid to try
something new.

Bob Hope

Security is mostly a superstition. It does not exist in nature… Life is either a daring adventure, or nothing.

Helen Keller

Learn how to be happy with what you have while you pursue all that you want.

Jim Rohn

Great work is done by
people who are not
afraid to be great.

Fernando Flores

Seize the moment.
Remember all those women
on the *Titanic* who waved off
the dessert cart.

Erma Bombeck

The longest journey begins
with a single step, not with a
turn of the ignition key.

Edward Abbey

Follow your dreams.
Just make sure to
have fun too.

Chris Brown

To love what you do and feel
that it matters, how could
anything be more fun?

Katharine Graham

Go for it now.
The future is promised
to no one.

Wayne Dyer

KEEP CALM AND DRINK UP

£4.99

ISBN: 978 1 84953 102 3

'*In victory, you deserve champagne; in defeat, you need it.*'

Napoleon Bonaparte

BAD ADVICE FOR GOOD PEOPLE.

Keep Calm and Carry On, a World War Two government poster, struck a chord in recent difficult times when a stiff upper lip and optimistic energy were needed again. But in the long run it's a stiff drink and flowing spirits that keep us all going.

Here's a book packed with proverbs and quotations showing the wisdom to be found at the bottom of the glass.

If you're interested in finding out more about our humour books, follow us on Twitter: @SummersdaleLOL

www.summersdale.com

KEEP
CALM
YOU'RE ONLY
21

KEEP
CALM
YOU'RE ONLY
21
KEEP
CALM
YOU'RE ONLY
21
KEEP
CALM
YOU'RE ONLY
21
KEEP
CALM
YOU'RE ONLY
21
KEEP
CALM
YOU'RE ONLY
21
KEEP
CALM
YOU'RE ONLY
21
KEEP
CALM
YOU'RE ONLY
21
KEEP
CALM
YOU'RE ONLY
21
KEEP
CALM
YOU'RE ONLY
21
KEEP
CALM
YOU'RE ONLY
21
KEEP
CALM
YOU'RE ONLY
21